The Secret Language of Plants Unlocking the Genetics and Genomics Behind Growth

Ezequiel Koa

Copyright © [2023]

Title: The Secret Language of Plants Unlocking the Genetics and Genomics Behind Growth
Author's: Ezequiel Koa

All rights reserved. No part of this publication may be reproduced, stored in a retrieval system, or transmitted in any form or by any means, electronic, mechanical, photocopying, recording, or otherwise, without the prior written permission of the publisher or author, except in the case of brief quotations embodied in critical reviews and certain other non-commercial uses permitted by copyright law.

This book was printed and published by [Publisher's: **Ezequiel Koa**] in [2023]

ISBN:

TABLE OF CONTENT

Chapter 1: Introduction to Plant Genetics and Genomics   07

The Importance of Studying Plant Genetics

The Role of Genomics in Understanding Plant Growth

Brief History of Plant Genetics and Genomics Research

Chapter 2: Fundamentals of Plant Genetics   13

DNA Structure and Function

Genes and Alleles

Mendelian Genetics and Inheritance Patterns

Chapter 3: Tools and Techniques in Plant Genetics and Genomics   19

DNA Extraction and Sequencing

Polymerase Chain Reaction (PCR)

Genome Mapping and Sequencing Technologies

Chapter 4: Understanding Plant Growth and Development 25

Plant Life Cycle: From Seed to Flowering

Hormonal Regulation of Plant Growth

Environmental Factors Influencing Plant Growth

Chapter 5: Genetic Variability in Plant Populations 31

Genetic Diversity and Its Importance

Gene Flow and Genetic Drift

Population Genetics and Plant Breeding

Chapter 6: Genomics and Crop Improvement 37

Genomic Approaches to Crop Improvement

Genetically Modified Organisms (GMOs) and Their Implications

Genomic Selection and Breeding Strategies

Chapter 7: Plant Genome Sequencing Projects 43

Overview of Major Plant Genome Sequencing Initiatives

Case Studies: Plant Species with Fully Sequenced Genomes

Comparative Genomics and Evolutionary Insights

Chapter 8: Applications of Plant Genetics and Genomics 49

Understanding Disease Resistance in Plants

Improving Yield and Nutritional Content

Conservation and Preservation of Endangered Plant Species

Chapter 9: Ethical Considerations in Plant Genetics and Genomics 55

Intellectual Property Rights and Patents

Ethics of Genetic Modification in Agriculture

Balancing Benefits and Risks in Plant Genomics Research

Chapter 10: Future Directions in Plant Genetics and Genomics   61

Advances in High-Throughput Sequencing Technologies

Integration of Omics Technologies in Plant Research

Potential Impact of Plant Genetics and Genomics on Sustainable Agriculture

Conclusion: Unlocking the Secrets of Plant Genetics and Genomics   67

Chapter 1: Introduction to Plant Genetics and Genomics

The Importance of Studying Plant Genetics

Subchapter: The Importance of Studying Plant Genetics

Introduction:

In today's world, where environmental concerns and food security are at the forefront, understanding plant genetics has become more crucial than ever before. From improving crop yields to developing disease-resistant plants, the study of plant genetics holds immense significance. This subchapter aims to shed light on the importance of studying plant genetics and its implications for everyone, particularly those interested in the fields of genetics and genomics.

1. Unveiling the Secrets of Evolution:

Studying plant genetics allows us to unravel the mysteries of evolution. By examining the genetic makeup of plants, scientists can trace their ancestry, discover their evolutionary history, and gain insights into how they have adapted to various environmental conditions over time. This knowledge not only helps us understand the past but also provides valuable information for predicting future changes in plant species.

2. Boosting Crop Yields:

As the world's population continues to grow, the demand for food is increasing exponentially. Studying plant genetics enables scientists to develop crops with higher yields, enhanced nutritional value, and improved resistance against pests, diseases, and environmental stresses. By manipulating plant genes, researchers can create varieties that are more productive, efficient, and sustainable, ultimately contributing to global food security.

3. Conservation and Biodiversity:

Plant genetics plays a vital role in the conservation of endangered plant species and the preservation of biodiversity. By studying the genetic diversity within plant populations, scientists can identify rare genes and traits that may be crucial for the survival of certain species. This knowledge helps in developing conservation strategies, ensuring that unique plant varieties are protected for future generations.

4. Medicinal and Industrial Applications:

Plants have been a source of medicines, fibers, and biofuels for centuries. Understanding plant genetics allows scientists to identify and manipulate genes responsible for producing valuable compounds, opening doors to new medical treatments, sustainable materials, and renewable energy sources. Studying plant genetics also helps in optimizing cultivation practices, leading to increased production and quality of plant-based products.

Conclusion:

The study of plant genetics is essential for everyone, especially those interested in the fields of genetics and genomics. It offers insights into evolution, helps boost crop yields, contributes to conservation efforts, and unlocks the potential for new medicinal and industrial applications. By understanding plant genetics, we can harness the power of nature to address pressing global challenges, ensuring a sustainable and prosperous future for all.

The Role of Genomics in Understanding Plant Growth

Plants have always fascinated scientists and researchers due to their incredible ability to grow, adapt, and survive in diverse environments. For centuries, we have been unraveling the mysteries of plant growth, attempting to understand the complex mechanisms that govern their development. In recent years, the field of genomics has emerged as a powerful tool in this pursuit, offering unprecedented insights into the genetic makeup of plants and their growth processes.

Genomics, a branch of genetics, focuses on studying the complete set of genes, known as the genome, within an organism. It involves mapping, sequencing, and analyzing the DNA of plants to understand their genetic composition and the functions of individual genes. By doing so, scientists can uncover the underlying molecular mechanisms that drive plant growth, development, and response to various stimuli.

One of the key applications of genomics in plant science is the identification of genes responsible for important traits such as yield, disease resistance, and stress tolerance. By studying the genomes of different plant species, scientists can pinpoint specific genes that contribute to these desirable traits and use this knowledge to develop improved varieties through selective breeding or genetic modification.

Genomics also plays a crucial role in understanding the regulatory networks that control plant growth. Through advanced techniques such as transcriptomics and proteomics, researchers can analyze the expression patterns of thousands of genes simultaneously. This enables them to identify genes that are activated or repressed during different stages of plant growth, shedding light on the complex interplay of genes and their products in various physiological processes.

Furthermore, genomics has revolutionized our understanding of plant evolution and biodiversity. By comparing the genomes of different plant species, scientists can trace their evolutionary history, identify common genetic elements, and unravel the genetic changes that have occurred over millions of years. This knowledge is invaluable for conservation efforts, crop improvement, and predicting how plants may respond to future environmental challenges.

In conclusion, genomics has emerged as a powerful tool in understanding plant growth and development. Its ability to unravel the secrets hidden within the plant genome has revolutionized our understanding of the molecular mechanisms that govern plant growth, as well as their evolution and response to the environment. By harnessing the power of genomics, we can unlock the genetic and genomic secrets of plants, paving the way for innovative strategies to enhance crop productivity, improve sustainability, and ensure food security for future generations.

Brief History of Plant Genetics and Genomics Research

In this subchapter, we will embark on an intriguing journey through the fascinating history of plant genetics and genomics research. From ancient civilizations to modern breakthroughs, the understanding of plant life and its genetic makeup has evolved significantly over the centuries.

The study of plant genetics traces its roots back to ancient times when early agricultural societies began to observe and manipulate plants for their own benefit. The ancient Egyptians, for instance, were pioneers in selective breeding, as they selectively crossed plants to produce desired traits. This simple yet groundbreaking practice laid the foundation for the future exploration of plant genetics.

Fast forward to the mid-19th century, when Gregor Mendel, an Austrian monk, conducted groundbreaking experiments with pea plants. Mendel's work on inheritance patterns revealed the existence of dominant and recessive genes, providing the first glimpse into the mechanisms of heredity. Although his discoveries were initially overlooked, they later became the cornerstone of modern genetics.

The field of plant genetics continued to advance in the early 20th century. Barbara McClintock, an American scientist, made significant contributions to our understanding of genetic recombination in corn, uncovering the presence of mobile genetic elements or "jumping genes." Her work challenged the prevailing dogma of the time and opened up new avenues of research, ultimately leading to the discovery of transposable elements.

In recent decades, the advent of genomics has revolutionized plant genetics research. Genomics, the study of an organism's entire genetic material, has allowed scientists to unravel the mysteries encoded within plant genomes. The completion of the Arabidopsis thaliana genome sequence in 2000 marked a major milestone in plant genomics, providing researchers with a valuable model organism for further investigations.

Furthermore, advancements in DNA sequencing technologies have made it possible to decode the genomes of various crop plants, such as rice, corn, and wheat. This wealth of genetic information has enabled scientists to identify key genes responsible for important agronomic traits, paving the way for the development of improved crop varieties through genetic modification and breeding programs.

In conclusion, the history of plant genetics and genomics research is a testament to humankind's relentless pursuit of understanding the intricate language of plants. From ancient civilizations to modern scientific breakthroughs, our knowledge of plant genetics has grown exponentially, revolutionizing agriculture and offering new possibilities for sustainable food production. As we delve deeper into the secrets of plant genetics and genomics, we unlock the potential to address global challenges and ensure a thriving future for both plants and humans.

Chapter 2: Fundamentals of Plant Genetics

DNA Structure and Function

DNA, or deoxyribonucleic acid, is the blueprint of life. It is a remarkable molecule that holds the key to our genetic makeup and determines the characteristics that make each of us unique. Understanding the structure and function of DNA is essential in unraveling the mysteries of life and unlocking the secrets of growth.

At its core, DNA is a double helix, resembling a twisted ladder. Its structure consists of two long strands made up of building blocks called nucleotides. These nucleotides are composed of a sugar molecule, a phosphate group, and one of four nitrogenous bases - adenine (A), thymine (T), cytosine (C), and guanine (G). The sequence of these bases along the DNA strand determines the genetic code for an organism.

The function of DNA is to store and transmit genetic information. It carries the instructions for building and maintaining an organism, passing on traits from one generation to the next. DNA achieves this through a process called replication, where the two strands separate, and each acts as a template for the creation of a new complementary strand. This ensures that every cell in our body contains the same genetic information.

Beyond replication, DNA is also responsible for protein synthesis. Genes, which are specific segments of DNA, contain the instructions for building proteins - the workhorses of our bodies. Through a process called transcription, the genetic information in a gene is copied into a molecule called messenger RNA (mRNA). This mRNA then travels to the ribosomes, where it serves as a template for protein synthesis.

The study of genetics and genomics has revolutionized our understanding of DNA and its role in growth and development. Through techniques such as DNA sequencing and genetic engineering, scientists can now decipher the entire genetic code of an organism and manipulate it to improve traits or solve genetic diseases.

Understanding the structure and function of DNA is not only important for scientists and researchers in the field of genetics and genomics but for everyone. It allows us to comprehend the fundamental principles of life and appreciate the incredible complexity of the natural world. By unlocking the secrets of DNA, we gain the power to shape the future of our own genetic destiny and the world around us.

Genes and Alleles

Genes and Alleles: Unraveling the Secrets of Plant Genetics

In the world of plants, a fascinating hidden language is constantly unfolding – the language of genes and alleles. Understanding this secret language is crucial for unlocking the mysteries behind the growth and development of plants. In this subchapter, we delve into the captivating world of genetics and genomics, exploring the intricacies of genes and alleles, and how they shape the vibrant tapestry of plant life.

At the very core of plant genetics lies the concept of genes. Genes are the fundamental units of heredity, carrying the instructions that guide the development and functioning of a plant. These instructions are encoded in the DNA molecules found within the cells of every plant.

By decoding the genetic information contained within these DNA molecules, scientists have been able to uncover the secrets of how plants grow, adapt, and evolve.

One key aspect of genes is the presence of different versions, known as alleles. Think of alleles as alternative versions of a gene that can influence specific traits or characteristics of a plant. For example, a gene controlling flower color may have different alleles, resulting in flowers of various hues. Alleles can be dominant, where their influence is readily visible, or recessive, where their effects are masked by dominant alleles.

The study of genes and alleles has led to remarkable breakthroughs in agricultural practices and crop improvement. By identifying and manipulating specific alleles, scientists can develop plants with desirable traits, such as disease resistance, higher yields, or enhanced nutritional value. This has significant implications for addressing global food security challenges and ensuring sustainable agriculture.

Genomics, on the other hand, is the study of an organism's entire set of genes, known as its genome. With the advent of advanced technologies, scientists can now sequence and analyze entire plant genomes, providing a comprehensive understanding of the genetic makeup of different species. This knowledge enables researchers to unravel the intricate networks of genes and alleles that contribute to plant growth, development, and adaptation.

The study of plant genetics and genomics is not only fascinating but also holds immense potential for the future. By deciphering the secret language of plants, scientists can improve crop productivity, develop resilient varieties, and contribute to environmental conservation efforts. Furthermore, understanding the genetic basis of plant traits can lead to novel discoveries in medicine, as many plant compounds have therapeutic properties.

In conclusion, the world of genes and alleles is a captivating realm, where the secret language of plants unfolds. By unraveling this language, scientists can gain insights into the complexities of plant growth and development, harnessing this knowledge for the benefit of humanity. Whether you are an enthusiast, a student, or a professional in the fields of genetics and genomics, exploring the hidden world of plant genetics promises to be an enlightening journey.

Mendelian Genetics and Inheritance Patterns

In the world of genetics and genomics, understanding the principles of Mendelian genetics and inheritance patterns is crucial. The study of how traits are passed from one generation to the next provides valuable insights into the secrets of plant growth and development. In this subchapter, we will explore the fascinating world of Mendelian genetics and its significance in unraveling the genetic language of plants.

Gregor Mendel, an Austrian monk, laid the foundation for modern genetics in the mid-19th century. His experiments with pea plants revealed that certain traits were inherited in predictable patterns. Mendel's work led to the discovery of dominant and recessive alleles, the units of heredity that determine specific traits. This groundbreaking research formed the basis of Mendelian genetics, which became the cornerstone of modern genetic studies.

One of the fundamental concepts in Mendelian genetics is the law of segregation. This law states that during the formation of gametes, the two alleles for a trait segregate from each other, ensuring that each gamete carries only one allele. This segregation allows for the recombination of genetic material during sexual reproduction, leading to the diversity we observe in plants and other organisms.

Another key principle is the law of independent assortment. This law proposes that different traits are inherited independently of each other. In other words, the inheritance of one trait does not influence the inheritance of another. This concept is vital for understanding how various traits are inherited and combined in offspring.

Understanding Mendelian genetics and inheritance patterns has numerous practical applications. Plant breeders, for instance, use this knowledge to selectively breed plants with desirable traits, such as disease resistance or increased yield. By understanding the patterns of inheritance, breeders can predict the likelihood of certain traits appearing in future generations, facilitating the development of improved plant varieties.

Moreover, Mendelian genetics plays a crucial role in genetic diseases and disorders. By studying patterns of inheritance, scientists can identify the genetic basis of these conditions and develop strategies for prevention, diagnosis, and treatment.

In conclusion, Mendelian genetics and inheritance patterns are the building blocks of our understanding of the genetic language of plants. By unraveling the principles outlined by Mendel, scientists and breeders gain insights into how traits are passed from one generation to the next. This knowledge has far-reaching implications, from improving crop productivity to combating genetic diseases. Embracing the secrets of Mendelian genetics allows us to unlock the potential hidden within the genetic and genomic makeup of plants, paving the way for a future of enhanced growth and development.

Chapter 3: Tools and Techniques in Plant Genetics and Genomics

DNA Extraction and Sequencing

In the ever-evolving field of genetics and genomics, one of the most crucial processes is DNA extraction and sequencing. This subchapter will delve into the fascinating world of unraveling the secrets hidden within the genetic code of plants. Whether you are a curious individual or a seasoned professional in the field, join us on this journey to unlock the mysteries behind growth.

DNA extraction is the first step in understanding the genetic makeup of any organism, including plants. It involves isolating the DNA molecules from the cells and tissues of the plant. This process allows scientists to study and manipulate the genetic material to gain insights into the plant's characteristics, behavior, and potential applications.

The extraction process starts by carefully selecting the plant material, whether it be leaves, stems, or even seeds. These plant samples are then treated with various reagents and enzymes to break down the cell walls and release the DNA. Once the DNA is liberated, it can be purified and concentrated, ready for further analysis.

Next comes the exciting process of DNA sequencing. This involves determining the specific order of the nucleotides (adenine, thymine, cytosine, and guanine) that make up the DNA molecule. Sequencing technologies have advanced significantly in recent years, allowing for faster and more accurate analysis of the genetic code.

By sequencing the DNA, scientists can identify and analyze specific genes responsible for various traits in plants. This crucial information can be used to understand how plants grow, adapt to their environment, and even defend themselves against diseases and pests. Furthermore, DNA sequencing enables researchers to compare the genetic makeup of different plant species, unveiling evolutionary relationships and identifying genetic variations that may have important implications for crop improvement and sustainability.

The applications of DNA extraction and sequencing in the field of genetics and genomics are vast. From developing disease-resistant crops to identifying new medicinal compounds, the knowledge gained through these techniques has the potential to revolutionize agriculture, medicine, and environmental conservation.

Whether you are a student, a researcher, or simply fascinated by the intricate world of genetics and genomics, understanding the process of DNA extraction and sequencing is essential. By peering into the secret language of plants, we can unlock the full potential of their genetics and genomics, paving the way for a more sustainable and prosperous future.

Polymerase Chain Reaction (PCR)

In the world of genetics and genomics, a powerful tool known as Polymerase Chain Reaction (PCR) has revolutionized the way scientists study and understand plants. This subchapter will delve into the intricacies of PCR, its principles, and its applications in unlocking the secrets of plant genetics.

PCR is a technique that allows scientists to make millions of copies of a specific DNA sequence, enabling them to amplify and study small amounts of DNA. This process involves a series of temperature changes that facilitate the replication of DNA in a test tube. By using a heat-stable DNA polymerase enzyme, such as Taq polymerase, scientists can repeatedly heat and cool a DNA sample to separate and replicate its strands. The result is an exponential increase in the number of DNA copies, making it easier for researchers to analyze and manipulate genetic material.

The applications of PCR in plant genetics are vast and diverse. It plays a vital role in identifying and characterizing plant genes, understanding their function, and even developing genetically modified organisms (GMOs) with improved traits. PCR can be used to detect specific DNA sequences, such as pathogens that cause plant diseases, allowing for quick and accurate identification. Additionally, PCR can assist in identifying genetic variations that contribute to desirable plant traits, aiding in the breeding of superior crops.

One of the most significant advancements in plant genetics made possible by PCR is the study of plant genomics. By sequencing and analyzing the entire DNA of a plant, scientists can gain insights into its genetic makeup, including the identification of genes responsible for various traits. PCR is a crucial component of this process, as it enables researchers to amplify and analyze specific regions of the plant's genome.

PCR has undoubtedly transformed the field of plant genetics and genomics. Its ability to amplify and manipulate DNA has opened doors to unprecedented discoveries and advancements. From identifying disease-causing pathogens to breeding superior crops, PCR has become an indispensable tool in the pursuit of understanding the secret language of plants.

Whether you are a genetics enthusiast or simply curious about the inner workings of plants, this subchapter on PCR will provide you with a glimpse into the exciting world of plant genetics and the powerful techniques that scientists employ to unravel their secrets. Join us as we explore the wonders of PCR and its profound impact on the field of genetics and genomics.

Genome Mapping and Sequencing Technologies

In the ever-evolving field of genetics and genomics, one of the most groundbreaking advancements has been the development of genome mapping and sequencing technologies. These cutting-edge tools have revolutionized our understanding of the secret language of plants and unlocked the mysteries behind their growth patterns.

Genome mapping involves determining the physical location of specific genes or DNA sequences on a plant's chromosomes. This process provides researchers with a detailed map of the plant's genetic makeup, allowing them to identify and study individual genes responsible for various traits or characteristics. By understanding the location of these genes, scientists can gain valuable insights into how plants grow, develop, and adapt to their environment.

Sequencing technologies take genome mapping a step further by unraveling the precise order of nucleotides within a plant's DNA. This process involves reading and decoding the genetic information contained in the DNA molecule. By sequencing a plant's genome, scientists can not only identify specific genes but also analyze the entire genetic code, providing a comprehensive view of the plant's genetic blueprint.

These technologies have revolutionized the study of genetics and genomics in plants. Researchers can now identify genes associated with desirable traits, such as disease resistance, drought tolerance, or increased yield. This information allows breeders to develop new varieties with improved characteristics, enhancing crop productivity and sustainability.

Genome mapping and sequencing technologies have also shed light on the intricate mechanisms of plant growth and development. By comparing the genomes of different plant species, scientists have discovered common genetic pathways and regulatory networks that govern fundamental processes like photosynthesis, flowering, and fruit ripening. This knowledge helps us understand how plants perceive and respond to environmental cues, paving the way for innovative strategies to optimize agricultural practices and mitigate the impact of climate change.

Moreover, these technologies have facilitated the identification of genetic variations within plant populations, leading to advancements in plant breeding and conservation efforts. By analyzing the genetic diversity present in crop plants, scientists can develop strategies to enhance resilience and adaptability, ensuring food security in the face of changing environmental conditions.

In conclusion, genome mapping and sequencing technologies have transformed our understanding of the genetics and genomics behind plant growth. These tools have empowered scientists to unravel the secret language of plants and decipher the complex mechanisms that drive their development. By harnessing this knowledge, we can unlock new opportunities for sustainable agriculture, improved crop varieties, and a deeper appreciation of the incredible world of plant genetics.

Chapter 4: Understanding Plant Growth and Development

Plant Life Cycle: From Seed to Flowering

Plants are an essential part of our ecosystem, providing us with oxygen, food, and beauty. But have you ever wondered how a tiny seed transforms into a magnificent flowering plant? In this subchapter, we delve into the fascinating journey of a plant's life cycle, unraveling the secrets behind its growth and development.

The life cycle of a plant begins with the seed. Seeds are nature's miracle packages, containing all the necessary genetic information and nutrients for a plant to grow. When conditions are favorable, such as adequate moisture, sunlight, and warmth, the seed germinates. This process initiates the growth of the embryonic plant, known as the seedling.

As the seedling emerges from the soil, it develops roots that anchor the plant, absorbing water and nutrients from the soil. Simultaneously, the shoot grows towards the sunlight, developing leaves that will play a crucial role in photosynthesis – the process by which plants convert sunlight into energy.

During the vegetative stage, the plant continues to grow and develop, focusing on building a strong foundation. It invests its energy in root and leaf development, preparing for the next phase of its life cycle. However, the transition from vegetative to reproductive growth is triggered by various environmental and genetic factors, such as the length of daylight and temperature.

Once the plant reaches maturity, it enters the flowering stage. This is the pinnacle of its life cycle, where it produces flowers. Flowers are remarkable structures that serve a vital purpose in reproduction. They contain male and female reproductive organs, enabling the plant to produce seeds through the process of pollination and fertilization.

During pollination, the transfer of pollen from the male reproductive organ (stamen) to the female reproductive organ (pistil) takes place. This can occur through various mechanisms, such as wind, water, insects, or animals. Once fertilization occurs, the plant begins to produce seeds, which carry the genetic information for future generations.

After the seeds are mature, the plant disperses them, ensuring their propagation and survival. This can be accomplished through various means, including wind, water, or animals. The cycle then starts anew as the seeds find their way to the soil and germinate, continuing the remarkable journey of plant life.

Understanding the genetics and genomics behind a plant's life cycle provides invaluable insights into how plants adapt, evolve, and interact with their environment. By unlocking these secrets, we can enhance agricultural practices, conserve endangered species, and even discover potential medicinal applications hidden within the plant kingdom.

Whether you are a gardening enthusiast, a biology student, or simply curious about the wonders of nature, exploring the plant life cycle is a fascinating journey that connects us to the intricate web of life on our planet. So, next time you admire a beautiful flower, take a moment to appreciate the incredible journey it took, from a tiny seed to a blooming wonder.

Hormonal Regulation of Plant Growth

In the fascinating world of plant biology, hormones play a vital role in regulating growth and development. Just like humans and animals, plants also possess a complex system of chemical messengers that coordinate various physiological processes. These hormones, known as phytohormones, control everything from seed germination to flowering and fruiting. Understanding the mechanisms by which plants regulate their growth through hormone signaling is essential for anyone interested in the fields of genetics and genomics.

One of the most well-known plant hormones is auxin. Auxin controls a wide range of plant growth processes, including cell elongation, root development, and tropisms (growth responses to external stimuli). By promoting cell elongation, auxin allows plants to grow towards light, enabling them to maximize photosynthesis. Additionally, it plays a crucial role in root formation and branching, enabling plants to efficiently absorb water and nutrients from the soil. The ability to manipulate auxin levels in plants has revolutionized agriculture, allowing for the development of dwarf varieties and faster, more robust crop growth.

Another essential hormone in plant growth regulation is gibberellin. Gibberellins are responsible for promoting stem elongation, seed germination, and flowering. Through its role in stem elongation, gibberellin allows plants to reach for sunlight and compete for resources. It also stimulates the breakdown of stored nutrients in seeds, triggering germination. Understanding gibberellin metabolism and signaling pathways has led to the development of techniques to control flowering time in crops, ensuring optimal yield and productivity.

Cytokinins are another class of hormones that play a crucial role in plant growth and development. Cytokinins promote cell division and differentiation, influencing leaf expansion, shoot formation, and the development of axillary buds. By regulating cytokinin levels, plants can adapt to changing environmental conditions and allocate resources for growth in specific areas. Manipulating cytokinin levels has proven useful in tissue culture and plant propagation, allowing for the mass production of disease-free plants.

Other plant hormones, such as abscisic acid, ethylene, and brassinosteroids, also contribute to the regulation of plant growth. Abscisic acid controls seed dormancy and stress responses, while ethylene influences fruit ripening and senescence. Brassinosteroids, on the other hand, are involved in cell elongation and stress tolerance.

Understanding the intricate network of hormonal regulation in plants is crucial for enhancing crop productivity, developing disease-resistant varieties, and mitigating the effects of climate change. By unraveling the genetic and genomic mechanisms behind hormone signaling, scientists can unlock the secrets of plant growth and revolutionize agriculture for a sustainable future. Whether you are a geneticist, a plant lover, or simply curious about the wonders of nature, delving into the hormonal regulation of plant growth will unveil a world of captivating discoveries.

Environmental Factors Influencing Plant Growth

Plants are essential for the well-being and survival of our planet. They provide oxygen, food, and shelter for various organisms, while also contributing to the overall balance of our ecosystems. However, plant growth is not solely determined by their genetic makeup; it is greatly influenced by environmental factors as well. Understanding these factors is crucial for anyone interested in the fields of genetics and genomics, as they play a significant role in shaping plant growth and development.

Light is one of the most critical environmental factors affecting plant growth. Through the process of photosynthesis, plants convert light energy into chemical energy, enabling them to produce food. Different plants have varying light requirements, with some thriving in full sun while others prefer shade. Understanding a plant's light requirements can help gardeners and researchers optimize their growth conditions.

Temperature is another vital factor affecting plant growth. Plants have specific temperature ranges in which they can grow optimally. Extreme heat or cold can stress plants, leading to reduced growth or even death. Knowing the temperature preferences of different plant species can aid in selecting suitable crops for specific regions or planning garden layouts.

Water availability is crucial for plant growth, as it is required for various physiological processes. Different plants have different water requirements, and understanding these needs is essential for proper irrigation and water management. Too much or too little water can hinder a plant's growth and even cause diseases such as root rot.

Soil composition and quality also greatly influence plant growth. The soil provides plants with essential nutrients and minerals necessary for their growth and development. Understanding the nutrient requirements of different plants can help ensure they receive adequate nourishment. Additionally, soil pH levels and texture can impact a plant's ability to absorb nutrients and water efficiently.

Other environmental factors that influence plant growth include air quality, humidity, and the presence of pollutants. Poor air quality, high pollution levels, or excessive humidity can negatively affect plant health and growth. Understanding these factors can help researchers develop strategies to mitigate their effects and create healthier environments for plants.

In conclusion, plant growth is influenced by a variety of environmental factors. Understanding these factors is essential for anyone interested in genetics and genomics, as they shape the growth and development of plants. By optimizing light, temperature, water, soil composition, and other environmental conditions, we can support healthy plant growth and ensure the well-being of our ecosystems.

Chapter 5: Genetic Variability in Plant Populations

Genetic Diversity and Its Importance

Genetic diversity, often referred to as the variety of genes within a particular species, is a fundamental aspect of life on our planet. It plays a crucial role in shaping the survival, adaptation, and evolution of species. From a single-celled organism to the majestic trees that dominate our forests, genetic diversity is the key to their resilience and ability to respond to environmental changes.

In the world of genetics and genomics, understanding and harnessing genetic diversity is of utmost importance. Every living organism carries a unique set of genes, and this diversity is what enables species to thrive in diverse ecosystems. The more diverse the gene pool, the greater the chances of survival and adaptation to environmental stresses, such as climate change, pathogens, and competition.

Genetic diversity is also vital for the stability of ecosystems. It ensures the availability of different traits and characteristics within a species, allowing them to respond to disturbances and maintain a balanced ecosystem. For instance, in a forest, trees with different genetic traits can withstand different types of pests or diseases, thus preventing a large-scale outbreak that could devastate the entire ecosystem.

Additionally, genetic diversity is essential for human survival and well-being. It underpins the development of crops that are resistant to pests, diseases, and adverse environmental conditions. Through selective breeding and genetic engineering, scientists can enhance genetic diversity and create more resilient and productive crops, ensuring food security for a growing global population.

Furthermore, genetic diversity holds great promise in the field of medicine. Individuals' unique genetic makeup influences their susceptibility to diseases, their response to medications, and their overall health. By studying genetic diversity, researchers can identify genetic variations associated with various diseases, paving the way for personalized medicine and targeted therapies.

Despite its importance, genetic diversity is under threat. Human activities, such as deforestation, habitat destruction, and the introduction of invasive species, have led to the loss of genetic diversity in many species. Conservation efforts, therefore, are crucial to preserving and restoring genetic diversity.

In conclusion, genetic diversity is the foundation of life and the key to the survival and adaptation of species. It is vital for the stability of ecosystems, food security, and the development of personalized medicine. Understanding and valuing genetic diversity is essential for both scientific advancements and maintaining the delicate balance of our planet's biodiversity. As stewards of this Earth, it is our responsibility to protect and nurture genetic diversity to ensure a sustainable and resilient future for all living organisms, including ourselves.

Gene Flow and Genetic Drift

In the intricate world of genetics and genomics, two fundamental concepts play a crucial role in shaping the genetic diversity of populations: gene flow and genetic drift. Understanding these processes is key to unraveling the mysteries hidden within the secret language of plants.

Gene flow refers to the movement of genes from one population to another. It occurs when individuals migrate or disperse, bringing their genetic material with them. This exchange of genes between populations can have profound effects on the genetic makeup of a species. By introducing new genetic variants, gene flow increases genetic diversity, promoting adaptation and evolution. It can also prevent populations from becoming genetically isolated, maintaining connectivity and allowing for the exchange of beneficial traits.

Genetic drift, on the other hand, is a random process that influences genetic variation within populations. It occurs when chance events, such as natural disasters or the random mating of individuals, lead to the loss or fixation of certain alleles. Genetic drift is particularly significant in small populations, where chance plays a more pronounced role. Over time, genetic drift can reduce genetic diversity and increase the frequency of certain alleles, potentially leading to the emergence of distinct populations.

Both gene flow and genetic drift shape the genetic landscape of plants, contributing to the rich tapestry of biodiversity we observe today. These processes have far-reaching implications, not only for the survival of plant species but also for human agriculture and conservation efforts.

For everyone interested in genetics and genomics, understanding the mechanisms of gene flow and genetic drift is crucial. By comprehending these fundamental concepts, we can grasp the underlying forces that drive genetic change in populations. This knowledge allows us to predict how plants will respond to environmental challenges, guide breeding programs to improve crop varieties, and develop effective strategies for preserving endangered plant species.

In the following chapters, we will delve deeper into the fascinating world of gene flow and genetic drift. We will explore the mechanisms that drive these processes, the factors that influence their magnitude, and the consequences they have on plant populations. Through this exploration, we will unlock the secrets hidden within the genetic code of plants, unraveling the mysteries of growth and adaptation. Join us on this journey of discovery as we decipher the secret language of plants and unlock the genetics and genomics behind their remarkable abilities.

Population Genetics and Plant Breeding

In the fascinating world of genetics and genomics, one area that holds immense significance is population genetics and plant breeding. This subchapter delves into the intricate relationship between these two fields and explores how they contribute to the understanding and enhancement of plant growth.

Population genetics is the study of genetic variation within populations of organisms. It seeks to unravel the factors that shape the genetic makeup of a population, including natural selection, genetic drift, migration, and mutation. By investigating the genetic diversity within a population, scientists can gain insights into the evolutionary processes at play and how they impact the survival and adaptability of plant species.

Plant breeding, on the other hand, is the deliberate manipulation of plant species to create desired traits. Through careful selection and controlled crossbreeding, plant breeders aim to enhance traits such as yield, disease resistance, and nutritional value. This process has played a pivotal role in the development of high-yielding crop varieties that feed the growing population.

Population genetics provides plant breeders with a fundamental understanding of the genetic diversity present within a population. By analyzing the gene pool of a particular plant species, breeders can identify desirable traits and genetic markers that can be used to guide their breeding programs. This knowledge allows breeders to make informed decisions and select parental plants that carry the desired genetic makeup, increasing the efficiency of the breeding process.

Furthermore, population genetics also assists in the conservation of plant biodiversity. By studying the genetic structure of wild populations, scientists can identify endangered species or genetic variants that possess unique traits. This information aids in the development of conservation strategies to protect and preserve these valuable genetic resources.

The combination of population genetics and plant breeding has revolutionized agriculture and horticulture. Through the utilization of advanced genomic technologies, breeders can now precisely manipulate the genetic makeup of plants to create novel varieties with improved traits. This has led to the development of disease-resistant crops, nutritionally enhanced fruits and vegetables, and environmentally sustainable agricultural practices.

In conclusion, population genetics and plant breeding form a powerful symbiotic relationship, driving the advancement of genetics and genomics in plant science. The integration of these fields enables scientists and breeders to unravel the secrets hidden within the genetic code of plants, leading to the development of innovative solutions for food security, sustainable agriculture, and the preservation of plant diversity. It is through this collaborative effort that we unlock the potential of plants and harness their genetic and genomic secrets for the betterment of humanity and our planet.

Chapter 6: Genomics and Crop Improvement

Genomic Approaches to Crop Improvement

In recent years, the field of genetics and genomics has revolutionized crop improvement, offering tremendous potential for enhancing agricultural productivity, sustainability, and food security. Through the application of advanced genomic techniques, scientists can now decipher the genetic codes of various crop species, enabling us to understand their growth processes and develop innovative strategies for crop improvement.

Genomic approaches to crop improvement involve studying and manipulating the complete set of genes, or the genome, of a particular crop species. This allows scientists to identify specific genes responsible for desirable traits such as increased yield, disease resistance, drought tolerance, or enhanced nutritional value. By understanding the genetic basis of these traits, breeders can then selectively breed or genetically engineer crops with these desired characteristics, resulting in improved varieties that can better adapt to changing environmental conditions or meet the nutritional needs of a growing population.

One of the key genomic tools used in crop improvement is high-throughput DNA sequencing. This technology enables scientists to rapidly sequence large amounts of DNA, providing a comprehensive view of the entire genome of a crop species. By comparing the genomes of different varieties or wild relatives of a crop, researchers can identify genetic variations that are associated with desirable traits. This information can then be used to develop molecular markers, which are DNA sequences that are closely linked to specific traits.

These markers serve as valuable tools for breeders, allowing them to select plants with the desired traits more efficiently and accurately.

Another important genomic approach is transcriptomics, which involves studying the complete set of RNA molecules produced by a crop's genes. By analyzing gene expression patterns, scientists can gain insights into how genes are regulated and identify key genes involved in important biological processes. This knowledge can be used to develop strategies for improving crop performance, such as enhancing photosynthesis efficiency or increasing nutrient uptake.

Furthermore, genomic approaches have also been instrumental in accelerating the development of genetically modified (GM) crops. By introducing specific genes into crop plants, scientists can confer desirable traits that are not naturally present in the species. For example, the introduction of genes for insect resistance in cotton or herbicide tolerance in soybeans has significantly reduced the need for chemical inputs, leading to more sustainable and environmentally friendly farming practices.

In conclusion, genomic approaches to crop improvement have revolutionized the field of agriculture, offering tremendous opportunities for enhancing crop productivity, sustainability, and nutritional value. By deciphering the genetic codes of crops and understanding the functions of their genes, scientists can develop innovative strategies for breeding or genetically engineering crops with improved traits. These advancements are critical in addressing the challenges of global food security, climate change, and sustainable agriculture, ensuring a brighter future for our planet and everyone who depends on it.

Genetically Modified Organisms (GMOs) and Their Implications

Genetically Modified Organisms (GMOs) have become a hot topic in recent years, sparking debates and discussions among scientists, policymakers, and the general public. In this subchapter, we will explore the fascinating world of GMOs and delve into their implications from a genetics and genomics perspective.

GMOs are organisms whose genetic material has been altered through genetic engineering techniques. This manipulation involves the introduction of foreign genes into an organism's DNA, resulting in new traits or characteristics that are not naturally found in the species. This process allows scientists to enhance certain desirable traits, such as increased crop yield, resistance to pests or diseases, or improved nutritional content.

One of the most significant implications of GMOs lies in their potential to revolutionize agriculture. By introducing genes that confer resistance to pests or extreme environmental conditions, scientists aim to develop crops that can thrive in challenging environments and provide higher yields. This has the potential to address food security issues and reduce the reliance on harmful pesticides and herbicides.

However, GMOs also raise concerns regarding their long-term effects on human health and the environment. Critics argue that the introduction of foreign genes into the food chain may have unpredictable consequences, such as allergenic reactions or the disruption of natural ecosystems. It is crucial to conduct thorough research and risk assessments to ensure the safety of GMOs before their widespread adoption.

From a genetic and genomic standpoint, GMOs offer valuable insights into the functioning of genes and their interactions. Studying the modifications made to an organism's genetic material can help us better understand gene expression, regulation, and the complex networks within living organisms. This knowledge can further our understanding of basic biological processes and pave the way for advancements in medicine, biotechnology, and environmental science.

As consumers, it is essential to be well-informed about GMOs and their implications. Understanding the science behind genetic modification empowers us to engage in informed discussions, make educated choices, and contribute to the ongoing debate surrounding GMOs. It is crucial to consider both the potential benefits and risks associated with GMOs and support transparent labeling practices, enabling individuals to make their own decisions based on their values and beliefs.

In conclusion, GMOs represent a significant advancement in the field of genetics and genomics. Their potential to address global challenges, such as food security and environmental sustainability, is undeniable. However, it is crucial to approach GMOs with caution, ensuring rigorous testing and regulation to minimize risks. By understanding the science and implications of GMOs, we can actively participate in shaping their future and harness their potential for the betterment of humanity and the planet.

Genomic Selection and Breeding Strategies

In the ever-evolving field of genetics and genomics, advancements in technology have revolutionized the way we understand and manipulate the genetic makeup of plants. One of the most powerful tools that has emerged is genomic selection, which allows breeders to make informed decisions when selecting plants for breeding programs. This subchapter will delve into the concept of genomic selection and explore the various breeding strategies that have been developed as a result.

Genomic selection is a method that uses high-throughput genotyping and phenotyping to identify and select plants with the most desirable traits for breeding purposes. By analyzing the entire genome of an individual plant, breeders can predict its genetic potential for specific traits, such as disease resistance, yield, or quality. This information enables breeders to make more accurate and efficient selections, saving time and resources compared to traditional phenotypic selection methods.

One of the key advantages of genomic selection is its ability to capture the genetic potential of plants at an early stage, even before they have fully expressed their traits. This allows breeders to make selections based on genetic markers associated with specific traits, rather than relying solely on observable characteristics. Furthermore, genomic selection can be applied to both conventional breeding and genetically modified organisms, providing a flexible approach to improve plant genetics.

In terms of breeding strategies, genomic selection has paved the way for new approaches that were previously unattainable. For example, marker-assisted selection (MAS) integrates genetic markers associated with desirable traits into the breeding process. By using these markers to guide selection decisions, breeders can accelerate the development of improved plant varieties.

Another strategy, genomic prediction, takes advantage of statistical models to predict the performance of a plant based on its genetic information. This allows breeders to estimate the breeding value of a plant even without extensive phenotypic data, making it particularly useful for traits that are difficult to measure or require multiple growing seasons.

In conclusion, genomic selection and the associated breeding strategies have revolutionized the field of genetics and genomics in plant breeding. By leveraging the power of genotyping and phenotyping, breeders can make informed decisions and accelerate the development of improved plant varieties. These advancements have the potential to address global challenges, such as food security and climate change, by producing crops with enhanced traits and resilience. Whether you are a genetics or genomics enthusiast or simply curious about the groundbreaking science behind plant breeding, the concept of genomic selection and its breeding strategies is an essential topic to explore.

Chapter 7: Plant Genome Sequencing Projects

Overview of Major Plant Genome Sequencing Initiatives

In recent years, plant genome sequencing initiatives have revolutionized the field of genetics and genomics, providing invaluable insights into the complex world of plant life. These initiatives have played a crucial role in unlocking the secrets of plant genetics and genomics, shedding light on the fundamental mechanisms behind growth and development. In this subchapter, we will provide an overview of some of the major plant genome sequencing projects that have significantly contributed to our understanding of plant biology.

One of the groundbreaking initiatives in this field is the International Rice Genome Sequencing Project (IRGSP). Rice, being a staple food for billions of people worldwide, has garnered immense scientific interest. The IRGSP successfully sequenced the rice genome, providing a comprehensive map of its DNA structure. This achievement has not only enhanced our understanding of rice genetics but also facilitated the development of improved varieties with enhanced traits such as disease resistance and higher yield.

Another remarkable initiative is the Arabidopsis Genome Initiative (AGI). Arabidopsis thaliana, a small flowering plant, has become a model organism for studying plant genetics due to its relatively simple genome and short life cycle. The AGI aimed to sequence the complete genome of Arabidopsis, resulting in the identification of thousands of genes responsible for various plant functions. This project has immensely contributed to our understanding of plant development, reproduction, and response to environmental cues.

The Maize Genome Sequencing Project (MGSP) stands as a significant milestone in plant genomics. Maize, also known as corn, is one of the most economically important crops globally. The MGSP unraveled the maize genome, revealing the genetic basis of various traits like drought tolerance, disease resistance, and nutritional content. This knowledge has paved the way for the development of genetically improved maize varieties, addressing global food security challenges.

Furthermore, the Human Genome Project (HGP), although primarily focused on human genetics, has greatly impacted plant genomics as well. This massive collaborative effort to sequence the human genome provided valuable insights into the similarities and differences between plant and human genomes. It highlighted the conservation of important genes and regulatory elements across different species, enabling scientists to better understand the genetic basis of various plant traits.

These major plant genome sequencing initiatives have expanded our knowledge of plant genetics and genomics, empowering researchers to explore new avenues in agricultural and environmental sciences. By deciphering the genetic code of plants, we are better equipped to develop innovative strategies for crop improvement, disease resistance, and sustainable agriculture. The implications of these initiatives extend beyond the scientific community, as they have the potential to shape the future of global food security and contribute to a more sustainable and resilient planet.

Case Studies: Plant Species with Fully Sequenced Genomes

In this subchapter, we will explore the fascinating world of plant genetics and genomics through a series of case studies on plant species with fully sequenced genomes. By understanding the genetic makeup of these plants, we can unlock the secrets behind their growth, development, and unique characteristics.

1. Arabidopsis thaliana: As one of the most extensively studied plant species, Arabidopsis thaliana has served as a model organism for plant genetics. Its small genome size and short life cycle make it ideal for studying the fundamental processes of plant growth and development. By fully sequencing its genome, scientists have gained insights into key genes and pathways that control various aspects of plant biology, including flowering time, hormone signaling, and stress responses.

2. Oryza sativa (Rice): With a fully sequenced genome, rice has proven to be a valuable resource for understanding not only its own biology but also that of other cereal crops. By comparing the rice genome to other crops, scientists have identified key genes and traits associated with important agronomic traits such as yield, disease resistance, and nutrient uptake. This knowledge has paved the way for crop improvement and breeding strategies to address global food security challenges.

3. Zea mays (Maize): As one of the most economically important crops worldwide, maize has been extensively studied and its genome fully sequenced. The maize genome is particularly interesting due to its large size and complex organization. By unraveling the maize genome, scientists have discovered important genes involved in kernel development, nitrogen utilization, and stress tolerance. This knowledge has revolutionized maize breeding programs, enabling the

development of improved varieties with higher yields and better nutritional content.

4. Solanum lycopersicum (Tomato): The fully sequenced genome of tomato has provided valuable insights into the biology and evolution of this popular crop. Researchers have identified genes responsible for traits such as fruit ripening, disease resistance, and flavor development. This knowledge has facilitated the development of improved tomato varieties with enhanced nutritional value, extended shelf life, and resistance to pests and diseases.

By studying these and other plant species with fully sequenced genomes, scientists have made significant strides in unraveling the genetic basis of plant growth and development. This information is not only valuable for basic research but also for practical applications such as crop improvement, conservation efforts, and the development of sustainable agriculture practices. Understanding the secret language encoded in plant genomes opens up a world of possibilities for harnessing the power of genetics and genomics to create a greener, more sustainable future for all.

Comparative Genomics and Evolutionary Insights

In the ever-expanding field of genetics and genomics, comparative genomics plays a crucial role in unraveling the mysteries of evolution. By studying the genomes of different species, scientists can gain valuable insights into the shared genetic heritage and the processes that have shaped life on Earth. This subchapter explores the fascinating world of comparative genomics and its implications for evolutionary biology.

Evolution, the driving force behind the diversity of life, is a complex process that operates through the accumulation and modification of genetic information. By comparing the genomes of different organisms, scientists can trace their evolutionary relationships and identify the changes that have occurred over millions of years. Through this comparative analysis, we can uncover the genetic mechanisms that have led to the emergence of new species and the adaptation of existing ones.

One of the key tools in comparative genomics is the identification of conserved genes and genomic regions. These are the sequences that have remained largely unchanged over long periods of evolutionary time, indicating their fundamental importance in the functioning of living organisms. By studying these conserved elements across species, scientists can uncover the basic building blocks of life and gain insights into the molecular processes that underpin biological functions.

Moreover, comparative genomics allows us to study the genetic basis of specific traits and diseases. By comparing the genomes of different organisms, scientists can identify the genes responsible for certain traits or diseases and understand their evolutionary history. This knowledge not only enhances our understanding of the genetic basis of complex traits but also opens up new avenues for medical research and the development of novel therapies.

In recent years, comparative genomics has been revolutionized by advances in DNA sequencing technologies. These groundbreaking techniques allow scientists to rapidly sequence the genomes of diverse organisms, providing an unprecedented wealth of data for comparative analysis. By combining these genomic data with computational approaches, researchers can now perform large-scale comparisons across species and gain deep insights into the evolutionary forces shaping life.

In conclusion, comparative genomics offers a powerful framework for understanding the genetic and genomic basis of evolution. By comparing the genomes of different species, scientists can uncover the shared genetic heritage and decipher the evolutionary processes that have shaped life on Earth. This knowledge not only deepens our understanding of biology but also has practical applications in fields such as medicine and agriculture. As we continue to unlock the secrets of the genetic and genomic language of plants and other organisms, the field of comparative genomics will undoubtedly play a pivotal role in our journey of discovery.

Chapter 8: Applications of Plant Genetics and Genomics

Understanding Disease Resistance in Plants

Disease resistance in plants is a complex and fascinating topic that plays a crucial role in the field of genetics and genomics. By unlocking the secrets behind disease resistance, scientists and researchers are able to develop strategies to combat plant diseases, increase crop yields, and ensure food security for the growing global population.

Plants, just like humans and animals, are susceptible to various diseases caused by pathogens such as bacteria, fungi, viruses, and nematodes. These diseases can have detrimental effects on plant growth, development, and overall health, leading to reduced crop yields and economic losses for farmers.

However, plants have evolved intricate defense mechanisms to protect themselves against these pathogens. These defense mechanisms are governed by a complex network of genes that regulate the plant's immune system. By studying the genetics and genomics behind disease resistance, scientists are able to gain insights into how plants recognize and respond to pathogens.

One of the key components of disease resistance in plants is the presence of resistance genes. These genes code for proteins that recognize specific pathogens and trigger an immune response in the plant. By identifying and studying these resistance genes, scientists can develop crops with enhanced disease resistance through genetic engineering or traditional breeding methods.

Furthermore, understanding the genetic basis of disease resistance allows scientists to develop diagnostic tools to detect and monitor plant diseases more effectively. This enables early detection and timely intervention, preventing the spread of diseases and minimizing crop losses.

In recent years, advancements in genetics and genomics technologies have revolutionized our understanding of disease resistance in plants. Techniques such as next-generation sequencing and genome editing have provided unprecedented opportunities to unravel the genetic basis of disease resistance and develop novel strategies to combat plant diseases.

In conclusion, understanding disease resistance in plants is of utmost importance in the field of genetics and genomics. By deciphering the secrets behind plant immunity, scientists and researchers can develop innovative solutions to combat plant diseases, increase crop yields, and ensure global food security. This knowledge not only benefits farmers and the agricultural industry but also has broader implications for human health and environmental sustainability.

Improving Yield and Nutritional Content

In the world of agriculture, the goal is not only to produce abundant crops but also to ensure that they are packed with essential nutrients. This subchapter will delve into the fascinating realm of improving yield and nutritional content in plants, exploring the intricate world of genetics and genomics that lies behind their growth.

Genetics plays a pivotal role in the development of plants with desirable traits, such as increased yield and enhanced nutritional content. Through careful selection and breeding, scientists have been able to improve crop characteristics over generations. However, recent advancements in genomics have revolutionized this process, allowing for more targeted and precise modifications.

One of the key tools in improving yield and nutritional content is genetic engineering. By introducing specific genes into plant genomes, scientists have been able to enhance traits such as disease resistance, drought tolerance, and increased productivity. For example, certain genes responsible for nitrogen fixation have been introduced into crops, enabling them to utilize atmospheric nitrogen and reduce the need for chemical fertilizers.

Furthermore, genomics has paved the way for a deeper understanding of the complex interactions between genes and nutrients. Scientists can now identify and manipulate genes responsible for the synthesis of essential vitamins, minerals, and other beneficial compounds in plants. This breakthrough knowledge has led to the development of biofortification techniques, where crops are engineered to contain higher levels of vitamins and minerals, addressing nutritional deficiencies that affect millions worldwide.

Additionally, genomics has enabled scientists to examine the intricate networks of genes and regulatory elements that control plant growth and development. By deciphering these genetic blueprints, researchers can fine-tune the expression of specific genes to optimize yield and nutrient content. This knowledge has led to the development of new breeding strategies and the identification of genetic markers that can accelerate the selection of desired traits in crops.

Improving yield and nutritional content is not only crucial for meeting the demands of a growing global population but also for ensuring food security and addressing malnutrition. The advancements in genetics and genomics have opened up exciting possibilities for designing crops with enhanced productivity and increased nutritional value. By harnessing the power of these technologies, we can pave the way for a more sustainable and nourished future for everyone.

Whether you have a general interest in genetics and genomics or are specifically involved in the agricultural sector, understanding the intricate relationship between plant genetics and the improvement of yield and nutritional content is vital. This subchapter will provide a comprehensive overview of the latest advancements in this field, delving into the fascinating world of genetic engineering, biofortification, and genomic insights that are shaping the future of agriculture.

Conservation and Preservation of Endangered Plant Species

In today's world, where climate change and human activities threaten the delicate balance of ecosystems, it is crucial to focus our attention on the conservation and preservation of endangered plant species. These plants play a vital role in maintaining the biodiversity of our planet, and their loss can have far-reaching consequences for both humans and other organisms. In this subchapter, we will explore the importance of protecting endangered plant species and the role of genetics and genomics in their preservation.

Endangered plant species are those that are at risk of becoming extinct due to various factors such as habitat loss, overexploitation, pollution, and climate change. The loss of these plants can disrupt entire ecosystems, leading to a decline in biodiversity and affecting the stability of our environment. It is therefore crucial that we take immediate action to protect and conserve these species.

Genetics and genomics play a significant role in the conservation and preservation of endangered plant species. Through the study of their genetic makeup, scientists can gain insights into their unique characteristics, identify their vulnerabilities, and develop effective strategies for their protection. Genetic analysis helps in understanding the population structure, genetic diversity, and gene flow of these species, which are essential for their long-term survival.

Conservation efforts often involve the establishment of protected areas, such as national parks or botanical gardens, where endangered plant species can be preserved in their natural habitats or under controlled conditions. These areas serve as a safe haven for these plants, ensuring their survival and providing opportunities for further scientific research.

Additionally, genetic technologies such as DNA sequencing and genomics can aid in the identification of specific genes responsible for traits that contribute to the survival and adaptation of endangered species. This knowledge can be utilized to develop conservation strategies, including selective breeding or genetic engineering, to enhance the resilience and genetic diversity of endangered plant populations.

Furthermore, collaboration between scientists, conservation organizations, and policymakers is crucial to ensure the successful conservation and preservation of endangered plant species. By raising awareness, implementing sustainable practices, and enacting protective legislation, we can collectively work towards a future where these plants thrive and contribute to the overall health of our planet.

In conclusion, the conservation and preservation of endangered plant species are of utmost importance to maintain the delicate balance of our ecosystems. Genetics and genomics provide valuable tools and insights that can aid in their protection, allowing us to unlock the secrets of these plants and ensure their survival for generations to come. It is a collective responsibility of every individual to contribute towards the preservation of these species and safeguard the biodiversity of our planet.

Chapter 9: Ethical Considerations in Plant Genetics and Genomics

Intellectual Property Rights and Patents

In the fast-evolving field of Genetics and Genomics, the protection of intellectual property rights is of paramount importance. With groundbreaking discoveries being made every day, scientists and researchers must safeguard their innovations and ensure that their hard work and dedication are duly recognized and protected. This subchapter aims to shed light on the significance of intellectual property rights and patents in the world of plant genetics and genomics.

Intellectual property rights refer to legal rights that are granted to individuals or organizations for their creations or inventions. These rights allow innovators to have exclusive control over their inventions for a certain period, ensuring that others cannot use, sell, or profit from their discoveries without permission. In the realm of genetics and genomics, intellectual property rights play a crucial role in encouraging innovation, fostering creativity, and driving scientific progress.

One of the primary ways to protect intellectual property in the field of genetics and genomics is through patents. A patent is a government-granted exclusive right that allows inventors to prevent others from using, making, or selling their invention without their permission. Patents provide inventors with a monopoly over their invention for a specified period, typically 20 years, during which they can exclusively exploit their creation.

Patents in plant genetics and genomics are particularly significant as they enable researchers to protect their novel plant varieties, genetically modified organisms (GMOs), and other innovative plant-based technologies. These patents not only safeguard the financial interests of the inventors but also incentivize further research and development, leading to the discovery of new and improved plant varieties that can benefit society at large.

However, the issue of intellectual property rights and patents in genetics and genomics is not without controversies. Some argue that patents can hinder scientific progress by restricting access to crucial genetic information and impeding further research. Others raise concerns about the monopolistic control that patents can grant to a few companies, potentially limiting the availability and affordability of essential genetic technologies.

Balancing the need for intellectual property protection with the principles of open science and accessibility is an ongoing challenge. It calls for a careful examination of the patent system and the establishment of fair regulations that strike a balance between incentivizing innovation and ensuring the free flow of scientific knowledge.

In conclusion, intellectual property rights and patents are vital in the field of genetics and genomics. They provide inventors with the recognition, protection, and financial incentives they deserve for their groundbreaking discoveries. However, the complexities surrounding these rights require ongoing dialogue and examination to ensure that the benefits of intellectual property protection extend to both innovators and the wider scientific community.

Ethics of Genetic Modification in Agriculture

In the realm of genetics and genomics, the ethics of genetic modification in agriculture is a topic that sparks intense debate and raises important questions about the future of our food systems. As advancements in technology allow scientists to manipulate the genetic makeup of plants and animals, it is crucial to address the ethical implications that arise from these practices.

Genetic modification in agriculture involves altering the genes of crops or livestock to enhance desirable traits such as increased yield, disease resistance, or improved nutritional content. Proponents argue that this technology has the potential to revolutionize agriculture by addressing global challenges like food security and climate change. Genetic modification can produce crops that are more resistant to pests, diseases, and extreme weather conditions, ultimately leading to higher yields and reduced reliance on harmful pesticides and fertilizers.

However, the ethics surrounding genetic modification in agriculture are not without controversy. Critics express concerns about the potential environmental impacts and the long-term effects on human health. They argue that genetically modified organisms (GMOs) may disrupt natural ecosystems, harm biodiversity, and contribute to the emergence of superweeds or superbugs that are resistant to traditional control methods. Additionally, some worry about the unknown consequences of consuming genetically modified foods, raising questions about allergenicity and the potential for unintended health effects.

The socioeconomic implications of genetic modification in agriculture also demand consideration. Critics argue that the concentration of power and control in the hands of a few multinational corporations can lead to the exploitation of small-scale farmers and threaten traditional farming practices. Furthermore, the patenting of genetically modified seeds raises concerns about access to genetic resources and the potential for corporate monopolies in the agricultural sector.

To navigate the ethics of genetic modification in agriculture, it is essential to engage in a broader dialogue that involves scientists, policymakers, farmers, consumers, and civil society. Transparency, informed consent, and rigorous risk assessments are crucial elements that should underpin the development and deployment of genetically modified crops and livestock. Public awareness and education about the benefits and risks of genetic modification are also vital to ensure a well-informed society.

In conclusion, the ethics of genetic modification in agriculture are complex and multifaceted. As we delve further into the world of genetics and genomics, it is crucial to weigh the potential benefits against the risks and consider the long-term implications for our environment, health, and society as a whole. By fostering an open and inclusive dialogue, we can strive towards a future where genetic modification in agriculture is guided by ethical principles and serves the best interests of both present and future generations.

Balancing Benefits and Risks in Plant Genomics Research

In the rapidly advancing field of plant genomics, researchers are unlocking the secrets hidden within the genetic makeup of plants. This groundbreaking research offers immense potential benefits for various industries, including agriculture, medicine, and environmental conservation. However, with great power comes great responsibility. The exploration of plant genomics also raises ethical and environmental concerns that must be carefully considered and addressed.

One of the most significant benefits of plant genomics research is its potential to revolutionize agriculture. By understanding the genetic traits that contribute to crop yield, disease resistance, and nutritional content, scientists can develop genetically modified crops that are more resilient, productive, and nutritious. This could help tackle global food security challenges and reduce reliance on harmful pesticides and fertilizers.

Moreover, plant genomics research holds promise for medical advancements. Many plants contain compounds with therapeutic properties, and by uncovering their genetic blueprint, scientists can better understand how these compounds are produced. This knowledge can lead to the development of new drugs and treatments for various diseases, benefiting human health worldwide.

Furthermore, plant genomics research can contribute to environmental conservation efforts. By studying the genetic diversity of plant species, scientists can identify endangered species, assess their vulnerability, and devise conservation strategies. This knowledge can also aid in restoring degraded ecosystems and preserving biodiversity, which is essential for the health of our planet.

While these potential benefits are exciting, it is crucial to acknowledge and mitigate the risks associated with plant genomics research. One of the main concerns is the unintended consequences of genetically modified organisms (GMOs). It is vital to conduct thorough risk assessments and ensure that GMOs are rigorously tested for safety before their release into the environment or consumption by humans or animals.

Additionally, the ethical implications of plant genomics research cannot be ignored. Questions arise around ownership of genetic information, access to genetic resources, and the potential exploitation of indigenous knowledge. Striking a balance between scientific progress and respecting the rights and values of different communities is crucial for responsible plant genomics research.

In conclusion, plant genomics research offers immense benefits for agriculture, medicine, and environmental conservation. However, it is essential to carefully consider and manage the associated risks and ethical concerns. By striking a balance between scientific progress and responsible practices, we can unlock the full potential of plant genomics research while safeguarding our environment, health, and societal values.

Chapter 10: Future Directions in Plant Genetics and Genomics

Advances in High-Throughput Sequencing Technologies

In recent years, the field of genetics and genomics has witnessed remarkable advancements in high-throughput sequencing technologies. These cutting-edge techniques have revolutionized the way we study and understand the genetics and genomics behind growth in plants. In this subchapter, we will explore the exciting world of high-throughput sequencing and its implications for the field.

High-throughput sequencing, also known as next-generation sequencing (NGS), is a powerful tool that allows scientists to rapidly sequence and analyze large quantities of DNA or RNA. This technology has significantly accelerated the pace of genomic research, enabling researchers to obtain vast amounts of genetic information in a fraction of the time it took with traditional sequencing methods.

One of the key advantages of high-throughput sequencing is its ability to generate massive amounts of data simultaneously. This has opened up new avenues of research, enabling scientists to study the entire genome of plants with unprecedented detail. By sequencing the entire genome, researchers can identify and analyze specific genes and genetic variations associated with growth traits, such as plant height, flowering time, and yield.

Moreover, high-throughput sequencing has also paved the way for the exploration of non-coding regions of the genome, which were previously overlooked. These non-coding regions, once considered "junk DNA," are now recognized to play crucial roles in gene regulation and plant development. High-throughput sequencing allows scientists to comprehensively study these regions, shedding light on their functional significance and their contribution to growth processes.

Another remarkable advancement in high-throughput sequencing is the development of single-cell sequencing technologies. Traditional sequencing methods rely on bulk DNA samples, which provide an average picture of genetic information from a mixture of cells. However, single-cell sequencing allows researchers to analyze the genetic material of individual cells, providing unprecedented insights into cellular heterogeneity and genetic diversity within plant tissues.

The application of high-throughput sequencing technologies has not only expanded our understanding of the genetic and genomic basis of plant growth but has also revolutionized plant breeding. By identifying specific genes associated with desirable growth traits, breeders can now develop new plant varieties with improved characteristics more efficiently and accurately.

In conclusion, high-throughput sequencing technologies have brought about a paradigm shift in the field of genetics and genomics, enabling scientists to explore the secret language of plants like never before. The ability to analyze vast amounts of genetic information and study non-coding regions and individual cells has provided unprecedented insights into the genetics and genomics behind growth. With these advancements, we are poised to unlock the full potential of plants and harness their genetic diversity to address pressing agricultural challenges and pave the way for a more sustainable future.

Integration of Omics Technologies in Plant Research

In recent years, the field of plant research has witnessed a remarkable revolution due to the integration of omics technologies. These technologies have paved the way for a deeper understanding of the genetics and genomics underlying plant growth and development. By unraveling the secret language of plants, researchers are gaining valuable insights into how these organisms function and interact with their environment.

Omics, a term derived from genomics, proteomics, and metabolomics, refers to the comprehensive study of biological molecules and their interactions within a cell or organism. By incorporating these technologies, scientists can now investigate the entire molecular landscape of plants, enabling a holistic approach to understanding their biology.

Genetics and genomics play a vital role in the integration of omics technologies in plant research. With the advent of high-throughput DNA sequencing, scientists can now unravel the genetic code of plants with unprecedented speed and accuracy. This has opened up possibilities for identifying genes responsible for crucial plant traits, such as disease resistance, drought tolerance, and yield enhancement.

Furthermore, the integration of genomics with proteomics and metabolomics has allowed scientists to explore the dynamic interplay between genes, proteins, and metabolites in plants. By studying the expression patterns of genes and the corresponding proteins and metabolites, researchers can decipher the molecular mechanisms that govern plant growth, development, and responses to environmental stimuli.

Omics technologies have also revolutionized plant breeding and crop improvement. With the ability to sequence entire plant genomes, breeders can now identify genetic variations associated with desirable traits and incorporate them into breeding programs. This has accelerated the development of improved crop varieties with enhanced yield, nutritional value, and resilience to biotic and abiotic stresses.

The integration of omics technologies in plant research has not only deepened our understanding of plant biology but also unlocked new opportunities for sustainable agriculture and food security. By elucidating the intricate genetic and molecular networks within plants, scientists can now engineer crops with improved traits, contributing to global efforts to address the challenges posed by a growing population and climate change.

In conclusion, the integration of omics technologies in plant research has ushered in a new era of understanding and manipulating the genetics and genomics behind plant growth. This multidimensional approach has provided researchers with unprecedented insights into the complex biological processes occurring within plants. With the potential to revolutionize agriculture and address global challenges, the integration of omics technologies is a breakthrough that holds immense promise for the future of plant research.

Potential Impact of Plant Genetics and Genomics on Sustainable Agriculture

In recent years, the field of plant genetics and genomics has made significant strides, revolutionizing our understanding of plant biology and its potential applications in agriculture. This subchapter aims to explore the potential impact of plant genetics and genomics on sustainable agriculture, presenting an overview of the key advancements and their implications for a diverse audience.

Sustainable agriculture is a pressing concern in today's world, as we face numerous challenges such as climate change, population growth, and declining natural resources. To address these issues, scientists and researchers have turned to plant genetics and genomics to develop innovative solutions that can enhance crop productivity, resilience, and nutritional value while minimizing environmental impact.

One of the most significant breakthroughs in plant genetics and genomics is the development of genetically modified organisms (GMOs). By introducing specific genes into plants, scientists have been able to enhance traits such as pest resistance, drought tolerance, and herbicide tolerance. These advancements have the potential to reduce the use of chemical pesticides, conserve water, and increase overall crop yields, thus contributing to sustainable agricultural practices.

Additionally, plant genetics and genomics have enabled the development of precision agriculture techniques. By understanding the genetic makeup of crops, researchers can optimize farming practices, tailoring them to individual plant needs. This includes precise fertilizer application, efficient water management, and targeted pest control, resulting in reduced resource usage and improved crop performance. Precision agriculture not only contributes to sustainability but also enhances economic viability for farmers.

Furthermore, plant genomics has paved the way for the development of biofortified crops. Through genetic engineering, scientists can enhance the nutritional content of crops, addressing widespread micronutrient deficiencies in certain regions. This breakthrough has the potential to combat malnutrition and improve public health, particularly in developing countries where access to diverse diets may be limited.

In conclusion, the potential impact of plant genetics and genomics on sustainable agriculture is immense. From genetically modified organisms to precision agriculture and biofortification, these advancements offer promising solutions to the challenges faced by the agricultural sector. By harnessing the power of genetics and genomics, we can create a more sustainable and resilient food system, ensuring food security for future generations.

Conclusion: Unlocking the Secrets of Plant Genetics and Genomics

In this captivating journey into the world of plant genetics and genomics, we have explored the fascinating realm of how plants grow and develop. From the ancient wisdom of traditional plant breeding to the cutting-edge advancements in genome sequencing, our understanding of the secret language of plants has expanded exponentially.

Throughout this book, we have witnessed the incredible power of plant genetics and genomics to transform agriculture, medicine, and the environment. By unraveling the complex genetic code of plants, scientists have been able to develop new varieties with enhanced traits such as disease resistance, increased yield, and improved nutritional content.

One of the key takeaways from this exploration is the realization of how interconnected all living organisms are. The intricate web of life, where every plant, animal, and microorganism plays a vital role, highlights the importance of preserving biodiversity and understanding the genetic diversity within plant populations.

Moreover, the study of plant genetics and genomics has opened doors to innovative solutions for global challenges such as climate change and food security. By identifying the genes responsible for stress tolerance and adapting plants to changing environmental conditions, we can develop resilient crops that can thrive in harsh climates and ensure food production for a growing population.

The potential of plant genetics and genomics extends beyond agriculture. The discovery of natural compounds produced by plants has revolutionized medicine, leading to the development of life-saving drugs. Understanding the genetic basis of these compounds allows us to harness their therapeutic potential and find new treatments for various diseases.

As we conclude this journey, it is clear that the secrets of plant genetics and genomics are far from being fully unlocked. The field continues to evolve rapidly, with new technologies and discoveries constantly pushing the boundaries of our knowledge. The integration of genetics, genomics, and other related disciplines will pave the way for further breakthroughs and innovation in the years to come.

In embracing the secrets of plant genetics and genomics, we empower ourselves to address the challenges of the future and unlock the full potential of nature's green miracles. By appreciating the intricate language of plants, we can coexist harmoniously with our botanical companions, ensuring a sustainable and prosperous future for all.

Whether you are a genetics and genomics enthusiast or simply curious about the world around you, this book has provided a glimpse into the hidden realms of plants. Let us continue to explore, learn, and marvel at the secrets that await us in the vast and enchanting world of plant genetics and genomics.

www.ingramcontent.com/pod-product-compliance
Lightning Source LLC
LaVergne TN
LVHW052003060526
838201LV00059B/3821